This planner belongs to :

____

2026

January

S	M	T	W	T	F	S
				1	2	3
4	5	6	7	8	9	10
11	12	13	14	15	16	17
18	19	20	21	22	23	24
25	26	27	28	29	30	31

February

S	M	T	W	T	F	S
1	2	3	4	5	6	7
8	9	10	11	12	13	14
15	16	17	18	19	20	21
22	23	24	25	26	27	28

March

S	M	T	W	T	F	S
1	2	3	4	5	6	7
8	9	10	11	12	13	14
15	16	17	18	19	20	21
22	23	24	25	26	27	28
29	30	31				

April

S	M	T	W	T	F	S
			1	2	3	4
5	6	7	8	9	10	11
12	13	14	15	16	17	18
19	20	21	22	23	24	25
26	27	28	29	30		

May

S	M	T	W	T	F	S
					1	2
3	4	5	6	7	8	9
10	11	12	13	14	15	16
17	18	19	20	21	22	23
24	25	26	27	28	29	30
31						

June

S	M	T	W	T	F	S
	1	2	3	4	5	6
7	8	9	10	11	12	13
14	15	16	17	18	19	20
21	22	23	24	25	26	27
28	29	30				

July

S	M	T	W	T	F	S
			1	2	3	4
5	6	7	8	9	10	11
12	13	14	15	16	17	18
19	20	21	22	23	24	25
26	27	28	29	30	31	

August

S	M	T	W	T	F	S
						1
2	3	4	5	6	7	8
9	10	11	12	13	14	15
16	17	18	19	20	21	22
23	24	25	26	27	28	29
30	31					

September

S	M	T	W	T	F	S
		1	2	3	4	5
6	7	8	9	10	11	12
13	14	15	16	17	18	19
20	21	22	23	24	25	26
27	28	29	30			

October

S	M	T	W	T	F	S
				1	2	3
4	5	6	7	8	9	10
11	12	13	14	15	16	17
18	19	20	21	22	23	24
25	26	27	28	29	30	31

November

S	M	T	W	T	F	S
1	2	3	4	5	6	7
8	9	10	11	12	13	14
15	16	17	18	19	20	21
22	23	24	25	26	27	28
29	30					

December

S	M	T	W	T	F	S
		1	2	3	4	5
6	7	8	9	10	11	12
13	14	15	16	17	18	19
20	21	22	23	24	25	26
27	28	29	30	31		

Year in Pixels

	J	F	M	A	M	J	J	A	S	O	N	D
1.												
2.												
3.												
4.												
5.												
6.												
7.												
8.												
9.												
10.												
11.												
12.												
13.												
14.												
15.												
16.												
17.												
18.												
19.												
20.												
21.												
22.												
23.												
24.												
25.												
26.												
27.												
28.												
29.												
30.												
31.												

Color Codes

Notes

January 2026

MONDAY	TUESDAY	WEDNESDAY	THURSDAY
			1
5	6	7	8
12	13	14	15
19	20	21	22
26	27	28	29

January 2026

FRIDAY	SATURDAY	SUNDAY	NOTES
2	3	4	○
			○
			○
			○
			○
9	10	11	○
			○
			○
			○
16	17	18	○
			○
			○
			○
			○
23	24	25	○
			○
			○
			○
			○
30	31		NOTES

February 2026

MONDAY	TUESDAY	WEDNESDAY	THURSDAY
2	3	4	5
9	10	11	12
16	17	18	19
23	24	25	26

February 2026

FRIDAY	SATURDAY	SUNDAY	NOTES
		1	○
			○
			○
			○
			○
6	7	8	○
			○
			○
			○
13	14	15	○
			○
			○
			○
			○
20	21	22	○
			○
			○
			○
			○
27	28		NOTES

March 2026

MONDAY	TUESDAY	WEDNESDAY	THURSDAY
2	3	4	5
9	10	11	12
16	17	18	19
23	24	25	26

March

2026

FRIDAY	SATURDAY	SUNDAY	NOTES
		1	○
6	7	8	○
13	14	15	○
20	21	22	○
27	28	29	30 / 31

April 2026

MONDAY	TUESDAY	WEDNESDAY	THURSDAY
		1	2
6	7	8	9
13	14	15	16
20	21	22	23
27	28	29	30

<table>
<tr><td colspan="3"># April</td><td>## 2026</td></tr>
<tr><td>FRIDAY</td><td>SATURDAY</td><td>SUNDAY</td><td>NOTES</td></tr>
<tr><td>3</td><td>4</td><td>5</td><td>○</td></tr>
<tr><td>10</td><td>11</td><td>12</td><td>○</td></tr>
<tr><td>17</td><td>18</td><td>19</td><td>○</td></tr>
<tr><td>24</td><td>25</td><td>26</td><td>○</td></tr>
<tr><td></td><td></td><td></td><td>NOTES</td></tr>
</table>

May 2026

MONDAY	TUESDAY	WEDNESDAY	THURSDAY
4	5	6	7
11	12	13	14
18	19	20	21
25	26	27	28

May 2026

FRIDAY	SATURDAY	SUNDAY	NOTES
1	2	3	○
			○
			○
			○
			○
8	9	10	○
			○
			○
			○
15	16	17	○
			○
			○
			○
			○
22	23	24	○
			○
			○
			○
			○
29	30	31	Notes

June 2026

MONDAY	TUESDAY	WEDNESDAY	THURSDAY
1	2	3	4
8	9	10	11
15	16	17	18
22	23	24	25
29	30		

June 2026

FRIDAY	SATURDAY	SUNDAY	NOTES
5	6	7	○
			○
			○
			○
			○
12	13	14	○
			○
			○
			○
19	20	21	○
			○
			○
			○
			○
26	27	28	○
			○
			○
			○
			○
			Notes

July 2026

MONDAY	TUESDAY	WEDNESDAY	THURSDAY
		1	2
6	7	8	9
13	14	15	16
20	21	22	23
27	28	29	30

July

FRIDAY	SATURDAY	SUNDAY	NOTES
3	4	5	○
			○
			○
			○
			○
10	11	12	○
			○
			○
			○
17	18	19	○
			○
			○
			○
			○
24	25	26	○
			○
			○
			○
			○
31			NOTES

August 2026

MONDAY	TUESDAY	WEDNESDAY	THURSDAY
3	4	5	6
10	11	12	13
17	18	19	20
24	25	26	27

August 2026

FRIDAY	SATURDAY	SUNDAY	NOTES
	1	2	○
			○
			○
			○
			○
7	8	9	○
			○
			○
			○
14	15	16	○
			○
			○
			○
			○
21	22	23	○
			○
			○
			○
			○
28	29	30	31

September 2026

MONDAY	TUESDAY	WEDNESDAY	THURSDAY
	1	2	3
7	8	9	10
14	15	16	17
21	22	23	24
28	29	30	

September 2026

FRIDAY	SATURDAY	SUNDAY	NOTES
4	5	6	○
			○
			○
			○
			○
11	12	13	○
			○
			○
			○
18	19	20	○
			○
			○
			○
			○
25	26	27	○
			○
			○
			○
			○
			NOTES

October 2026

MONDAY	TUESDAY	WEDNESDAY	THURSDAY
			1
5	6	7	8
12	13	14	15
19	20	21	22
26	27	28	29

October 2026

FRIDAY	SATURDAY	SUNDAY	NOTES
2	3	4	○
			○
			○
			○
			○
9	10	11	○
			○
			○
			○
16	17	18	○
			○
			○
			○
			○
23	24	25	○
			○
			○
			○
			○
30	31		NOTES

November 2026

MONDAY	TUESDAY	WEDNESDAY	THURSDAY
2	3	4	5
9	10	11	12
16	17	18	19
23	24	25	26

November 2026

FRIDAY	SATURDAY	SUNDAY	NOTES
		1	○
6	7	8	○
13	14	15	○
20	21	22	○
27	28	29	30

December 2026

MONDAY	TUESDAY	WEDNESDAY	THURSDAY
	1	2	3
7	8	9	10
14	15	16	17
21	22	23	24
28	29	30	31

December 2026

FRIDAY	SATURDAY	SUNDAY	NOTES
4	5	6	○
			○
			○
			○
			○
11	12	13	○
			○
			○
			○
18	19	20	○
			○
			○
			○
			○
25	26	27	○
			○
			○
			○
			○
			NOTES

01 MONDAY

02 TUESDAY

03 WEDNESDAY

04 FRIDAY

December
2025

05 FRIDAY

06 SATURDAY

07 SUNDAY

08 MONDAY

09 TUESDAY

10 WEDNESDAY

11 THURSDAY

12 FRIDAY

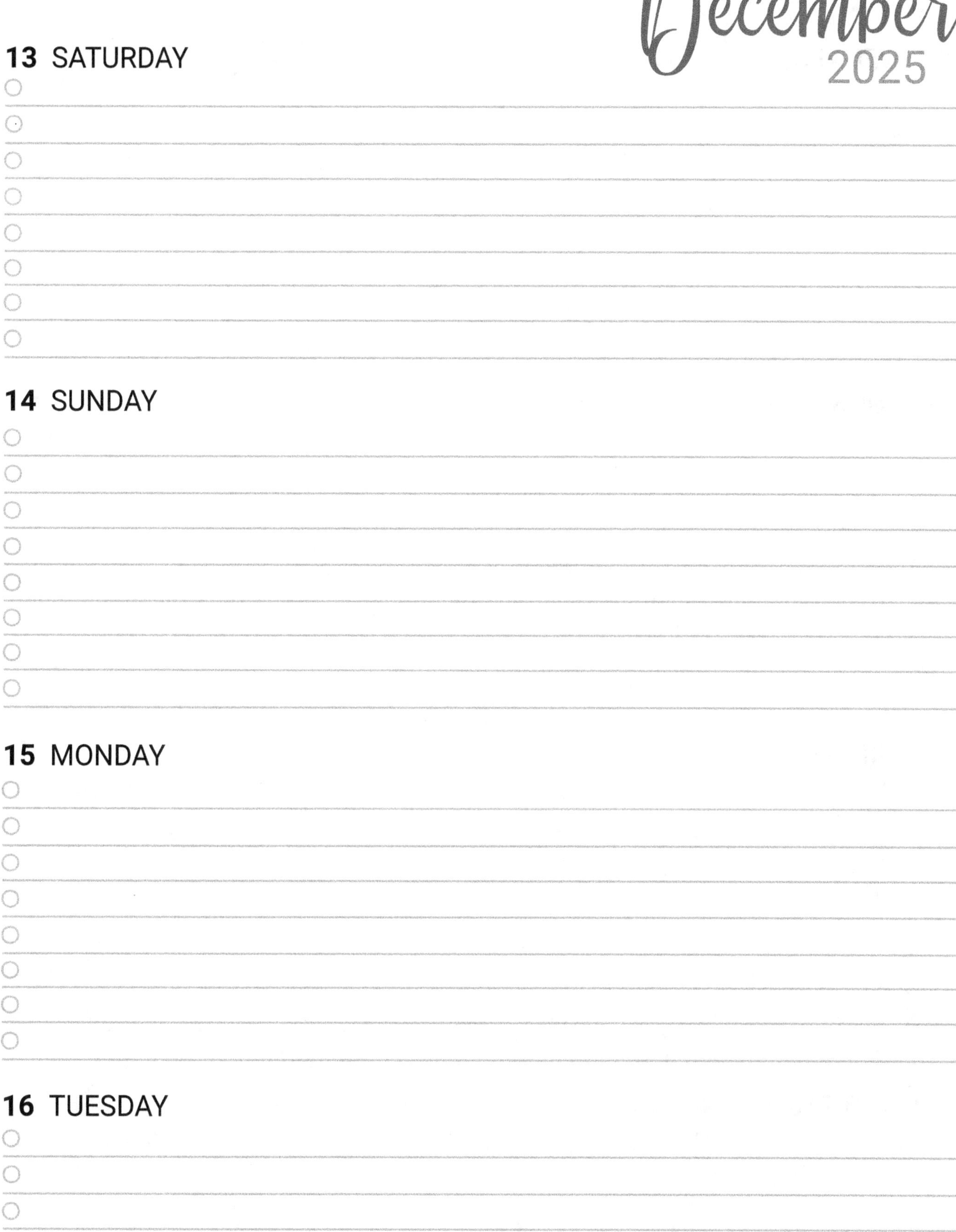

13 SATURDAY

14 SUNDAY

15 MONDAY

16 TUESDAY

17 WEDNESDAY

18 THURSDAY

19 FRIDAY

20 SATURDAY

December
2025

21 SUNDAY

22 MONDAY

23 TUESDAY

24 WEDNESDAY

25 THURSDAY

26 FRIDAY

27 SATURDAY

28 SUNDAY

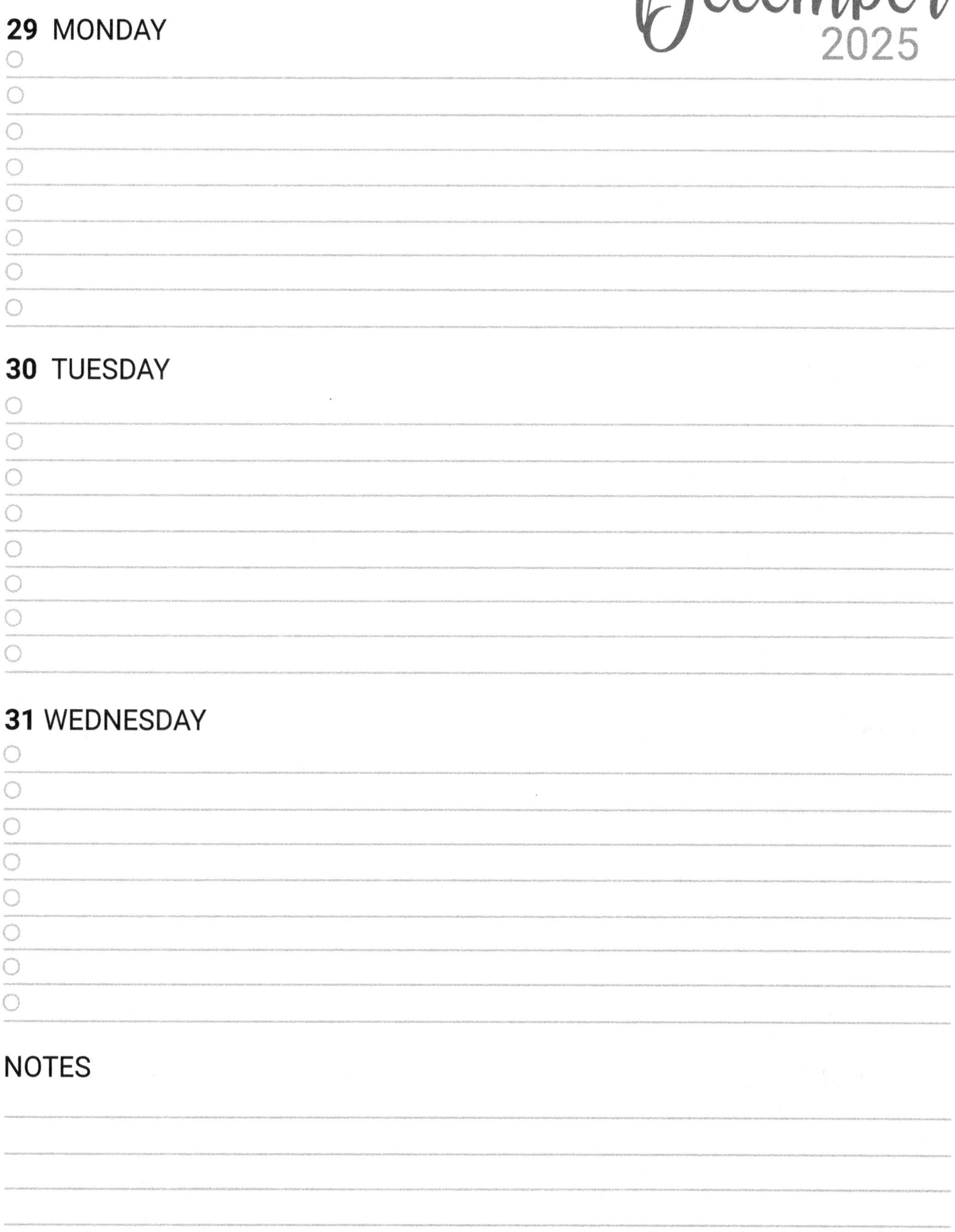

December
2025

29 MONDAY

30 TUESDAY

31 WEDNESDAY

NOTES

01 THURSDAY

02 FRIDAY

03 SATURDAY

04 SUNDAY

05 MONDAY

06 TUESDAY

07 WEDNESDAY

08 THURSDAY

09 FRIDAY

10 SATURDAY

11 SUNDAY

12 MONDAY

13 TUESDAY

14 WEDNESDAY

15 THURSDAY

16 FRIDAY

17 SATURDAY

18 SUNDAY

19 MONDAY

20 TUESDAY

January
2026

21 WEDNESDAY

22 THURSDAY

23 FRIDAY

24 SATURDAY

25 SUNDAY

26 MONDAY

27 TUESDAY

28 WEDNESDAY

29 THURSDAY

○
○
○
○
○
○
○
○

30 FRIDAY

○
○
○
○
○
○
○
○

31 SATURDAY

○
○
○
○
○
○
○
○

NOTES

01 SUNDAY

02 MONDAY

03 TUESDAY

04 WEDNESDAY

05 THURSDAY

06 FRIDAY

07 SATURDAY

08 SUNDAY

09 MONDAY

10 TUESDAY

11 WEDNESDAY

12 THURSDAY

13 FRIDAY

14 SATURDAY

15 SUNDAY

16 MONDAY

February
2026

17 TUESDAY

18 WEDNESDAY

19 THURSDAY

20 FRIDAY

21 SATURDAY

22 SUNDAY

23 MONDAY

24 TUESDAY

25 WEDNESDAY

26 THURSDAY

27 FRIDAY

28 SATURDAY

01 SUNDAY

02 MONDAY

03 TUESDAY

04 WEDNESDAY

05 THURSDAY

06 FRIDAY

07 SATURDAY

08 SUNDAY

09 MONDAY

10 TUESDAY

11 WEDNESDAY

12 THURSDAY

March
2026

13 FRIDAY

14 SATURDAY

15 SUNDAY

16 MONDAY

17 TUESDAY

18 WEDNESDAY

19 THURSDAY

20 FRIDAY

March
2026

21 SATURDAY

22 SUNDAY

23 MONDAY

24 TUESDAY

25 WEDNESDAY

26 THURSDAY

27 FRIDAY

28 SATURDAY

March
2026

29 SUNDAY

30 MONDAY

31 TUESDAY

NOTES

April 2026

01 WEDNESDAY

02 THURSDAY

03 FRIDAY

04 SATURDAY

April
2026

05 SUNDAY

06 MONDAY

07 TUESDAY

08 WEDNESDAY

09 THURSDAY

10 FRIDAY

11 SATURDAY

12 SUNDAY

13 MONDAY

14 TUESDAY

15 WEDNESDAY

16 THURSDAY

17 FRIDAY

18 SATURDAY

19 SUNDAY

20 MONDAY

21 TUESDAY

22 WEDNESDAY

23 THURSDAY

24 FRIDAY

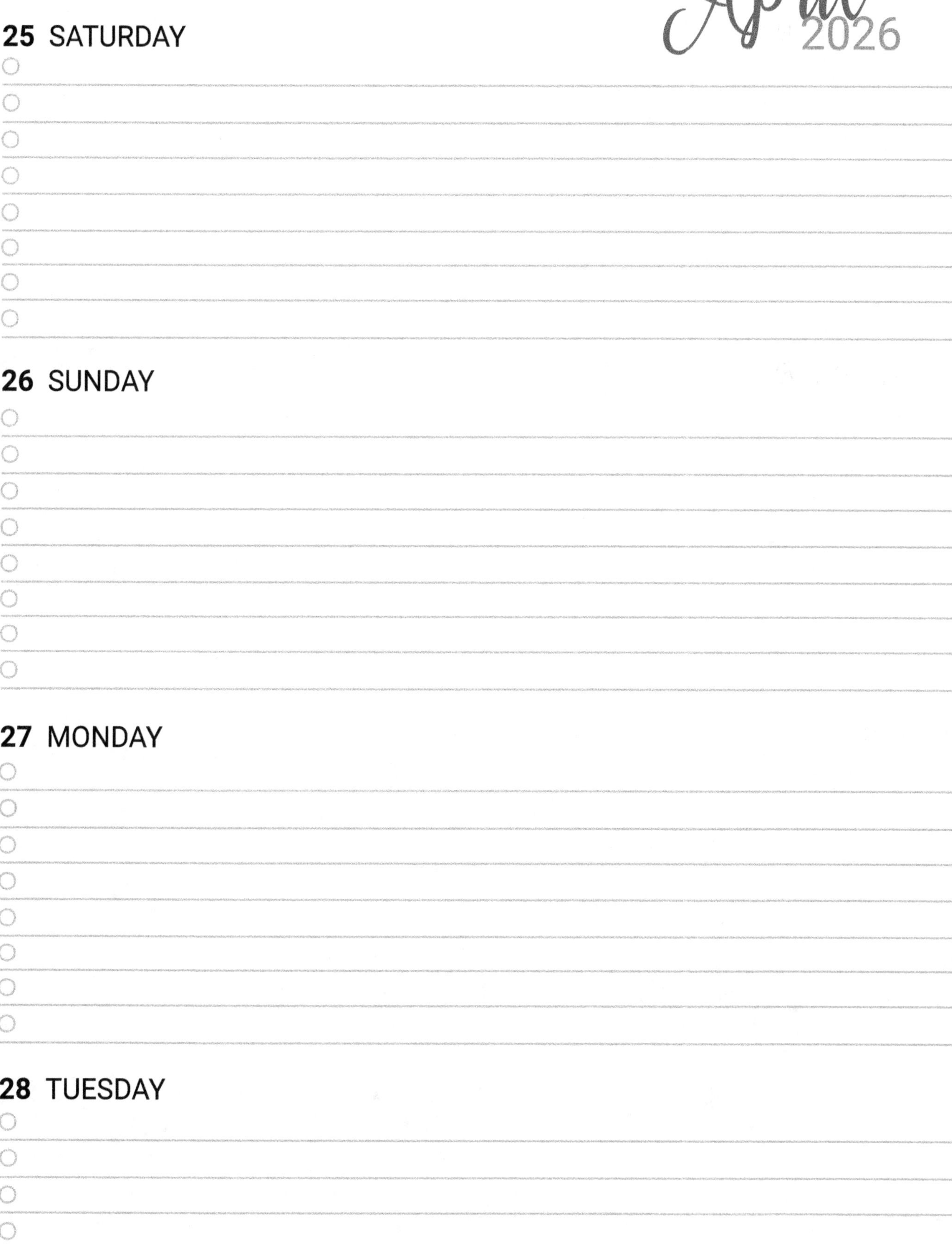

25 SATURDAY

26 SUNDAY

27 MONDAY

28 TUESDAY

29 WEDNESDAY

30 THURSDAY

NOTES

01 FRIDAY

02 SATURDAY

03 SUNDAY

04 MONDAY

05 TUESDAY

06 WEDNESDAY

07 THURSDAY

08 FRIDAY

09 SATURDAY

10 SUNDAY

11 MONDAY

12 TUESDAY

May 2026

13 WEDNESDAY

14 THURSDAY

15 FRIDAY

16 SATURDAY

May
2026

17 SUNDAY

18 MONDAY

19 TUESDAY

20 WEDNESDAY

21 THURSDAY

22 FRIDAY

23 SATURDAY

24 SUNDAY

May
2026

25 MONDAY

26 TUESDAY

27 WEDNESDAY

28 THURSDAY

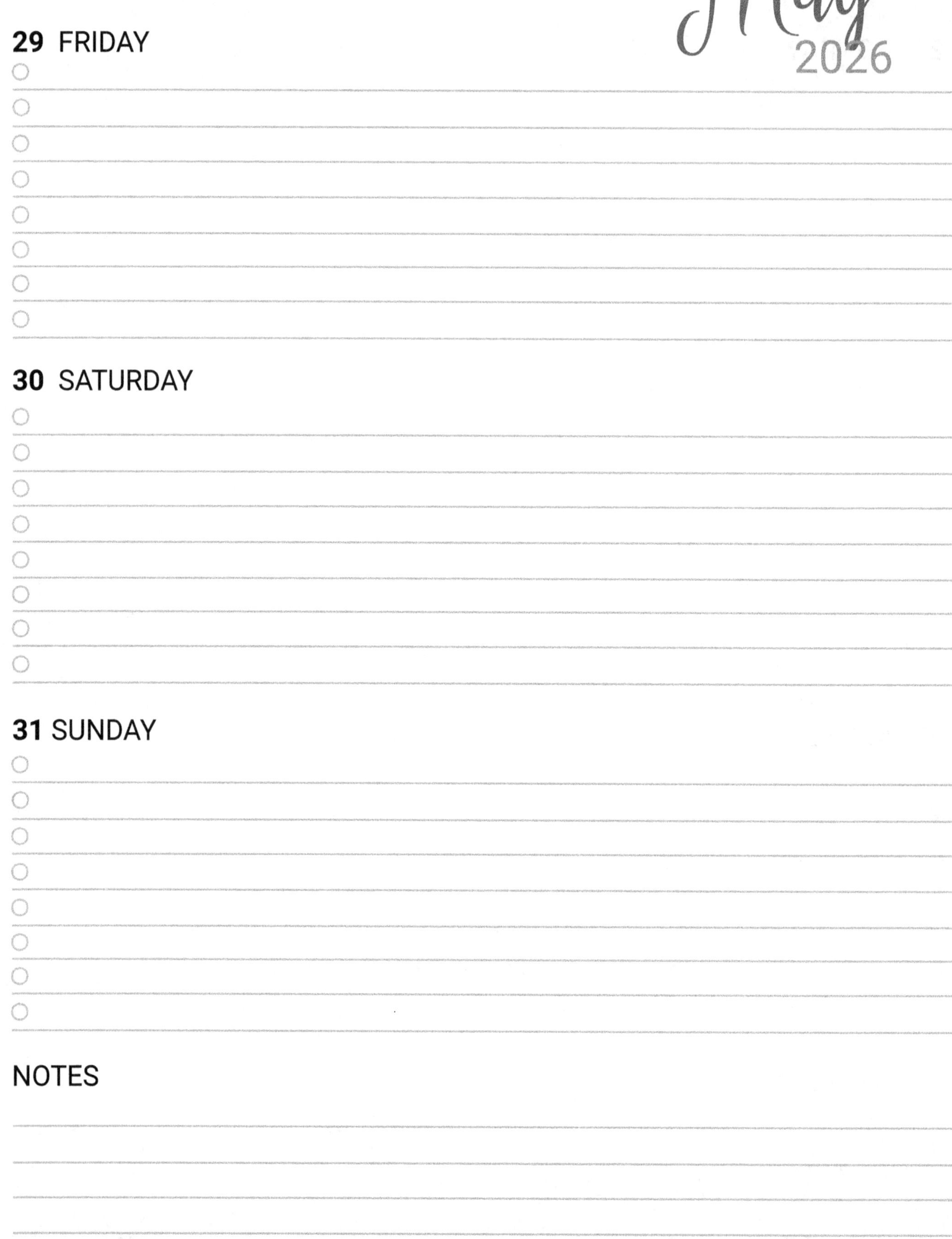

May
2026

29 FRIDAY

30 SATURDAY

31 SUNDAY

NOTES

01 MONDAY

02 TUESDAY

03 WEDNESDAY

04 THURSDAY

June
2026

05 FRIDAY

06 SATURDAY

07 SUNDAY

08 MONDAY

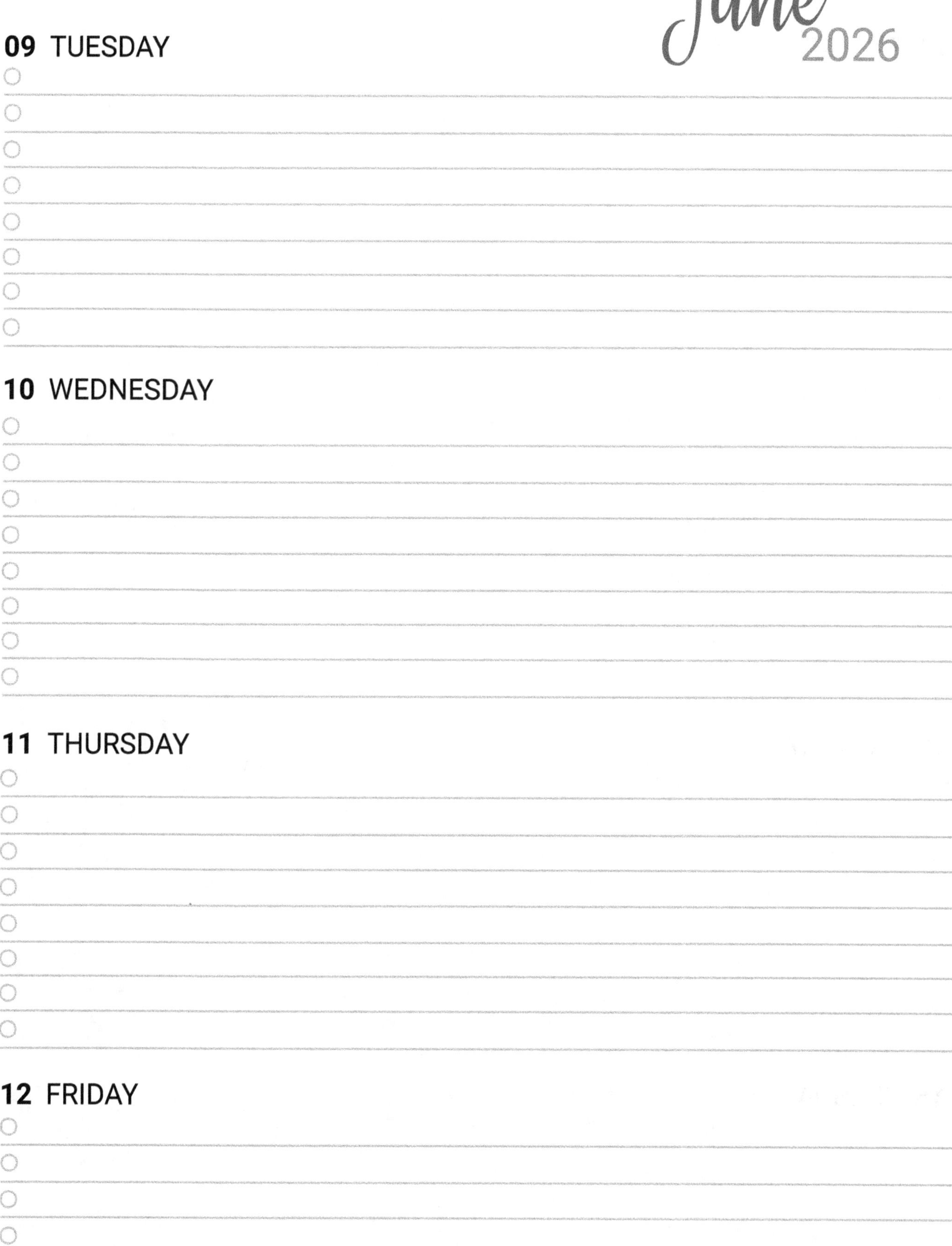

June 2026

09 TUESDAY

10 WEDNESDAY

11 THURSDAY

12 FRIDAY

13 SATURDAY

14 SUNDAY

15 MONDAY

16 TUESDAY

17 WEDNESDAY

18 THURSDAY

19 FRIDAY

20 SATURDAY

21 SUNDAY

22 MONDAY

23 TUESDAY

24 WEDNESDAY

25 THURSDAY

26 FRIDAY

27 SATURDAY

28 SUNDAY

29 MONDAY

○
○
○
○
○
○
○
○

30 TUESDAY

○
○
○
○
○
○
○
○

NOTES

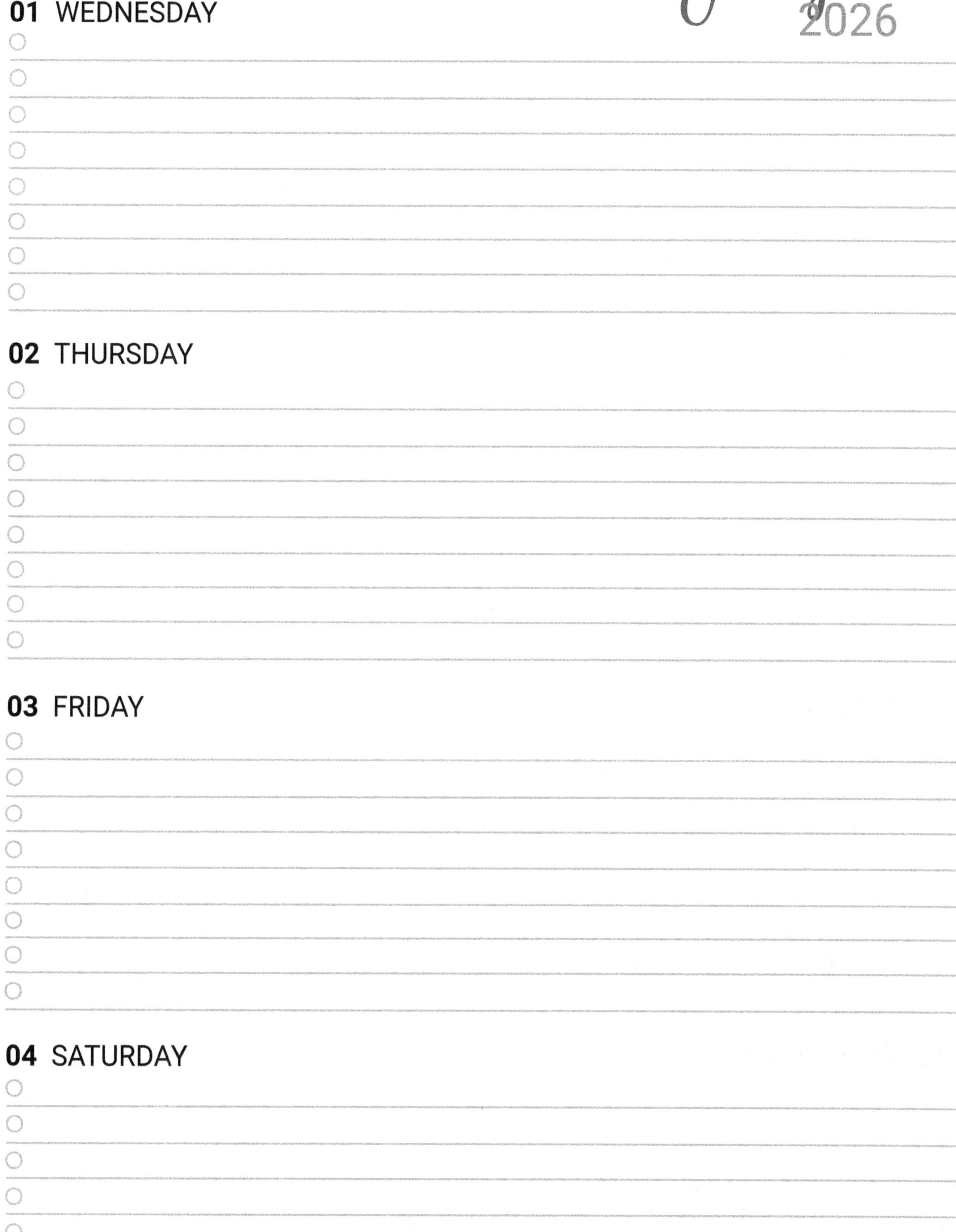

01 WEDNESDAY

02 THURSDAY

03 FRIDAY

04 SATURDAY

July
2026

05 SUNDAY

06 MONDAY

07 TUESDAY

08 WEDNESDAY

July
2026

09 THURSDAY

10 FRIDAY

11 SATURDAY

12 SUNDAY

13 MONDAY

14 TUESDAY

15 WEDNESDAY

16 THURSDAY

17 FRIDAY

18 SATURDAY

19 SUNDAY

20 MONDAY

21 TUESDAY

22 WEDNESDAY

23 THURSDAY

24 FRIDAY

25 SATURDAY

26 SUNDAY

27 MONDAY

28 TUESDAY

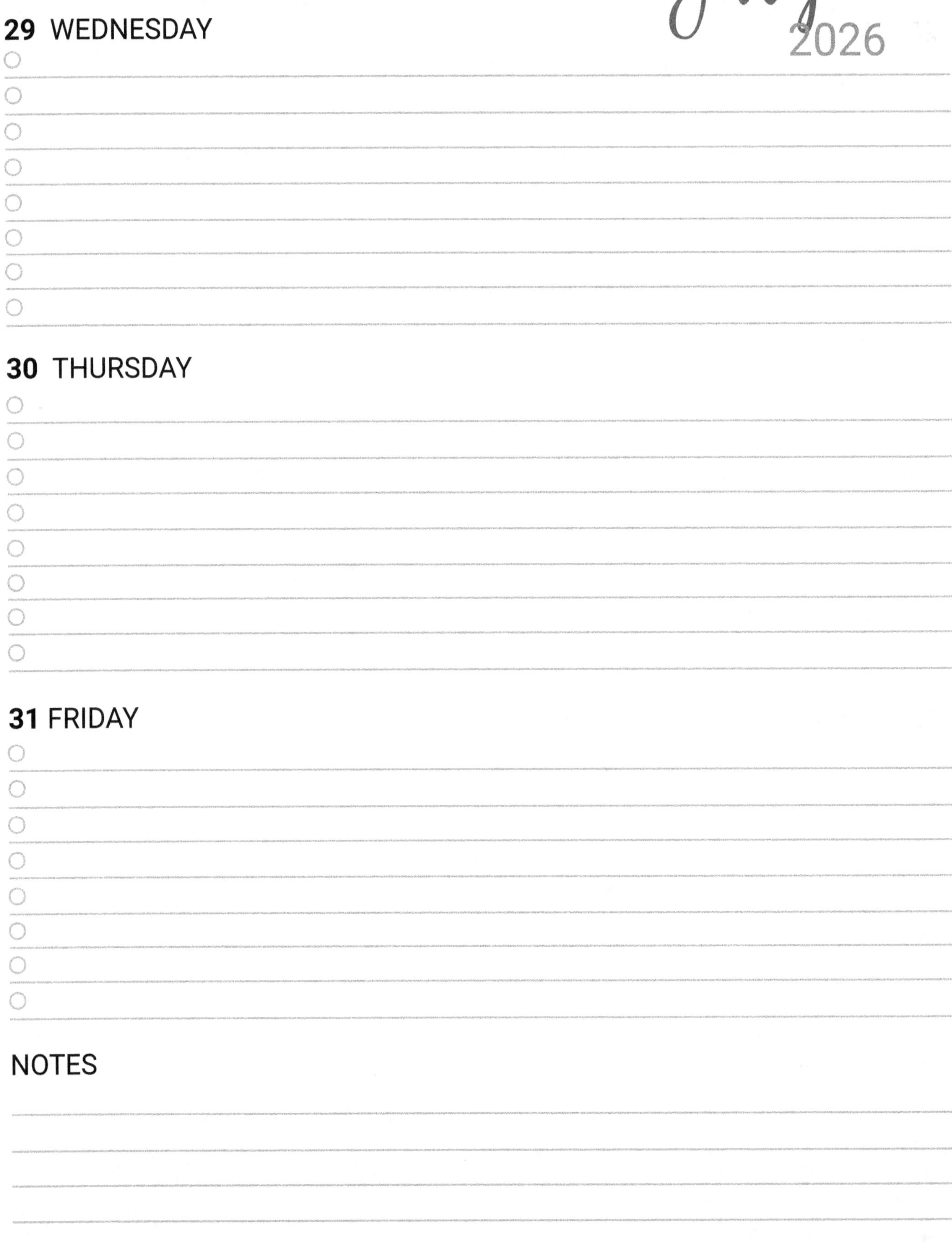

29 WEDNESDAY

30 THURSDAY

31 FRIDAY

NOTES

August
2026

01 SATURDAY

02 SUNDAY

03 MONDAY

04 TUESDAY

05 WEDNESDAY

06 THURSDAY

07 FRIDAY

08 SATURDAY

09 SUNDAY

10 MONDAY

11 TUESDAY

12 WEDNESDAY

13 THURSDAY

14 FRIDAY

15 SATURDAY

16 SUNDAY

August
2026

17 MONDAY

18 TUESDAY

19 WEDNESDAY

20 THURSDAY

August
2026

21 FRIDAY

22 SATURDAY

23 SUNDAY

24 MONDAY

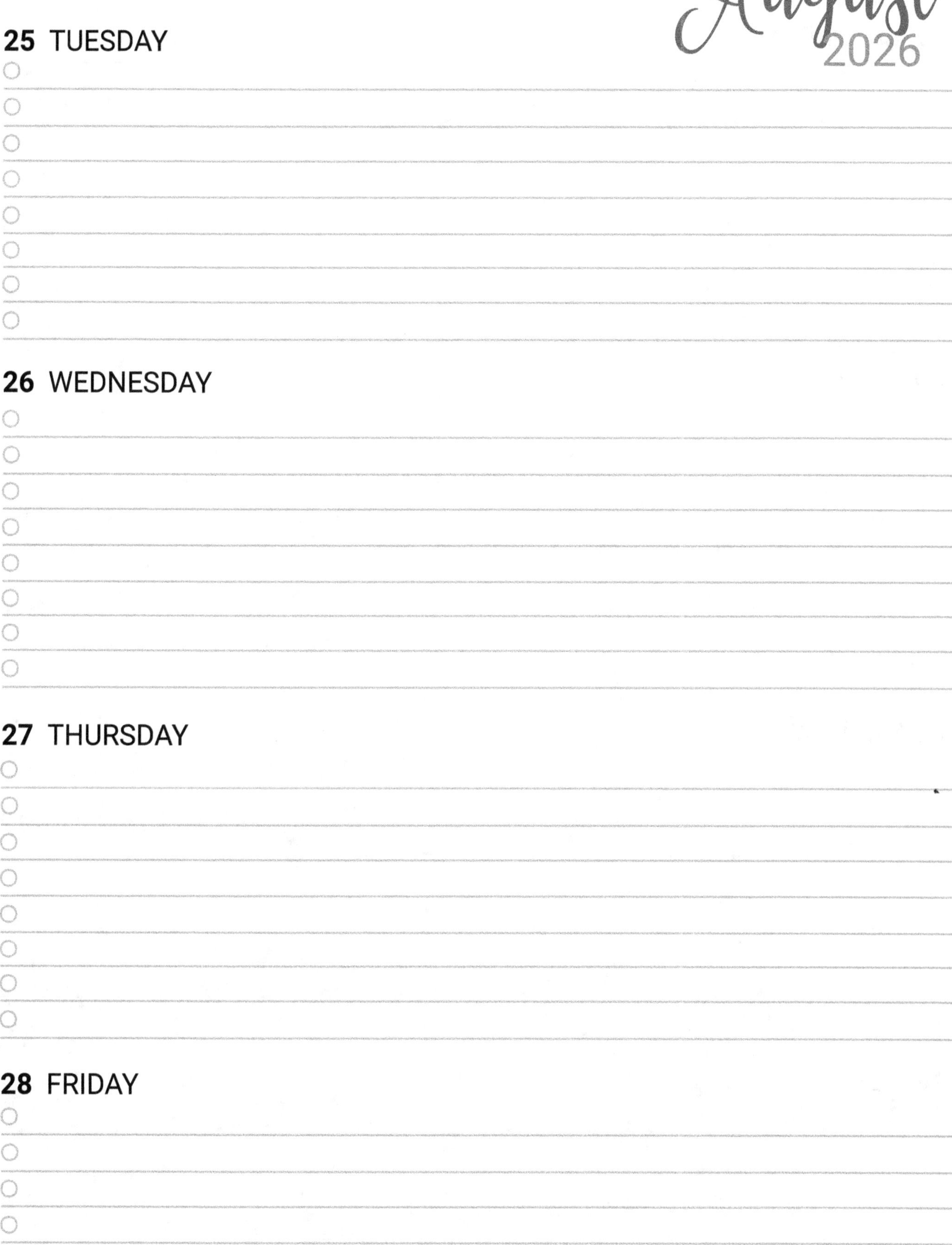

25 TUESDAY

26 WEDNESDAY

27 THURSDAY

28 FRIDAY

29 SATURDAY

30 SUNDAY

31 MONDAY

NOTES

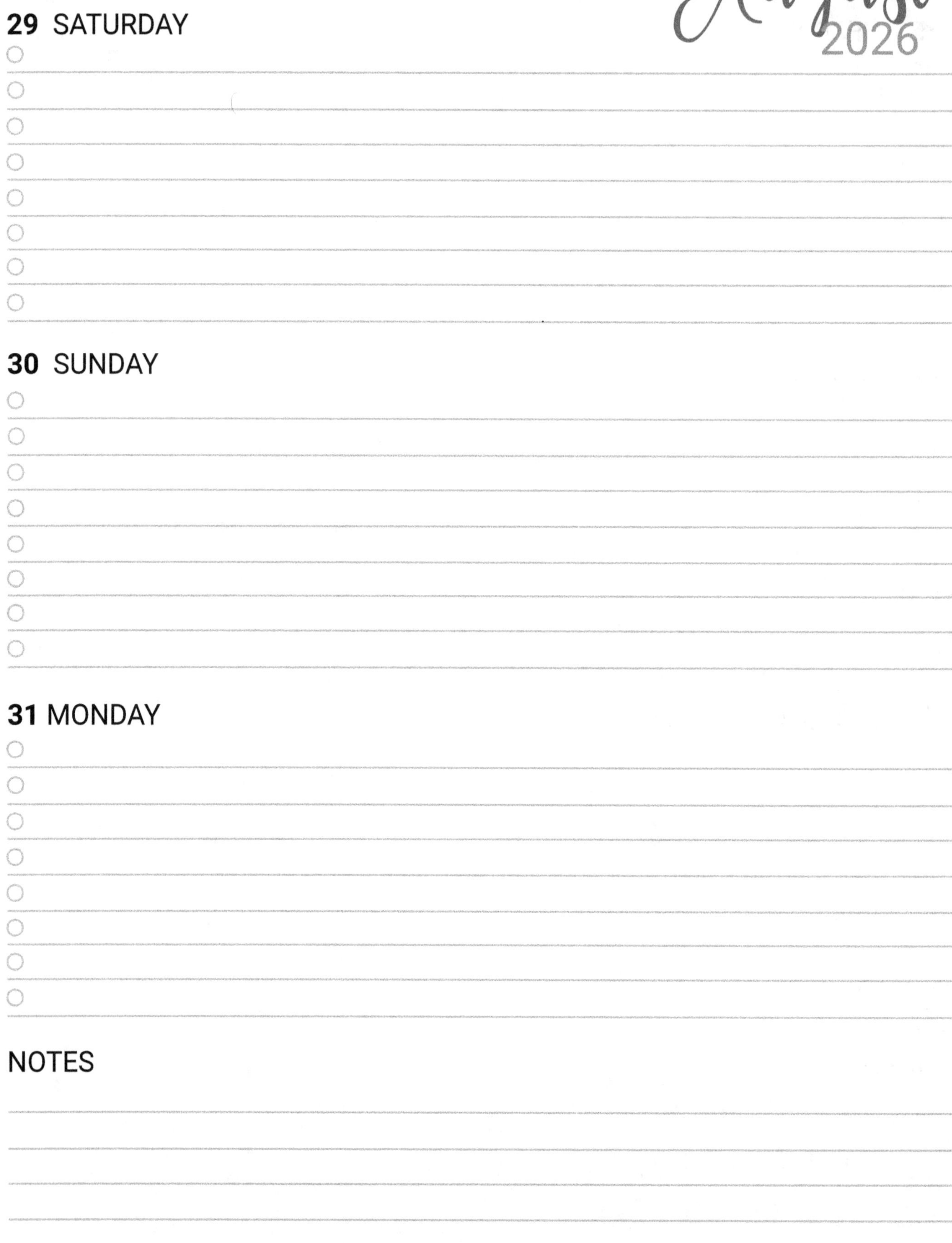

01 TUESDAY

02 WEDNESDAY

03 THURSDAY

04 FRIDAY

05 SATURDAY

06 SUNDAY

07 MONDAY

08 TUESDAY

09 WEDNESDAY

10 THURSDAY

11 FRIDAY

12 SATURDAY

13 SUNDAY

14 MONDAY

15 TUESDAY

16 WEDNESDAY

September
2026

17 THURSDAY

-
-
-
-
-
-
-
-

18 FRIDAY

-
-
-
-
-
-
-
-

19 SATURDAY

-
-
-
-
-
-
-
-

20 SUNDAY

-
-
-
-
-

21 MONDAY

22 TUESDAY

23 WEDNESDAY

24 THURSDAY

25 FRIDAY

26 SATURDAY

27 SUNDAY

28 MONDAY

29 TUESDAY

○
○
○
○
○
○
○
○

30 WEDNESDAY

○
○
○
○
○
○
○
○

NOTES

October
2026

01 THURSDAY

02 FRIDAY

03 SATURDAY

04 SUNDAY

05 MONDAY

06 TUESDAY

07 WEDNESDAY

08 THURSDAY

October
2026

09 FRIDAY

10 SATURDAY

11 SUNDAY

12 MONDAY

October
2026

13 TUESDAY

14 WEDNESDAY

15 THURSDAY

16 FRIDAY

October
2026

17 SATURDAY

18 SUNDAY

19 MONDAY

20 TUESDAY

21 WEDNESDAY

22 THURSDAY

23 FRIDAY

24 SATURDAY

October
2026

25 SUNDAY

26 MONDAY

27 TUESDAY

28 WEDNESDAY

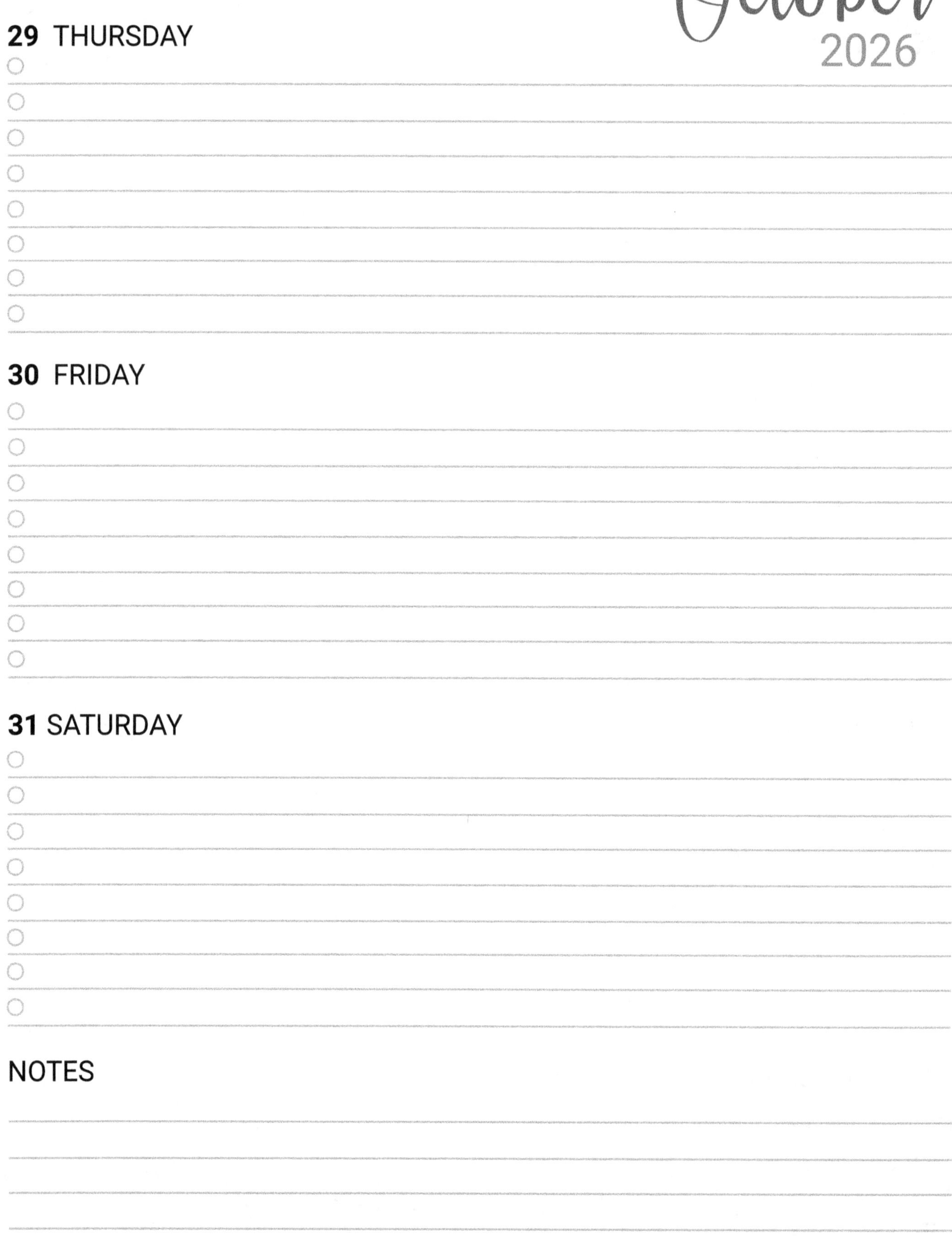

29 THURSDAY

30 FRIDAY

31 SATURDAY

NOTES

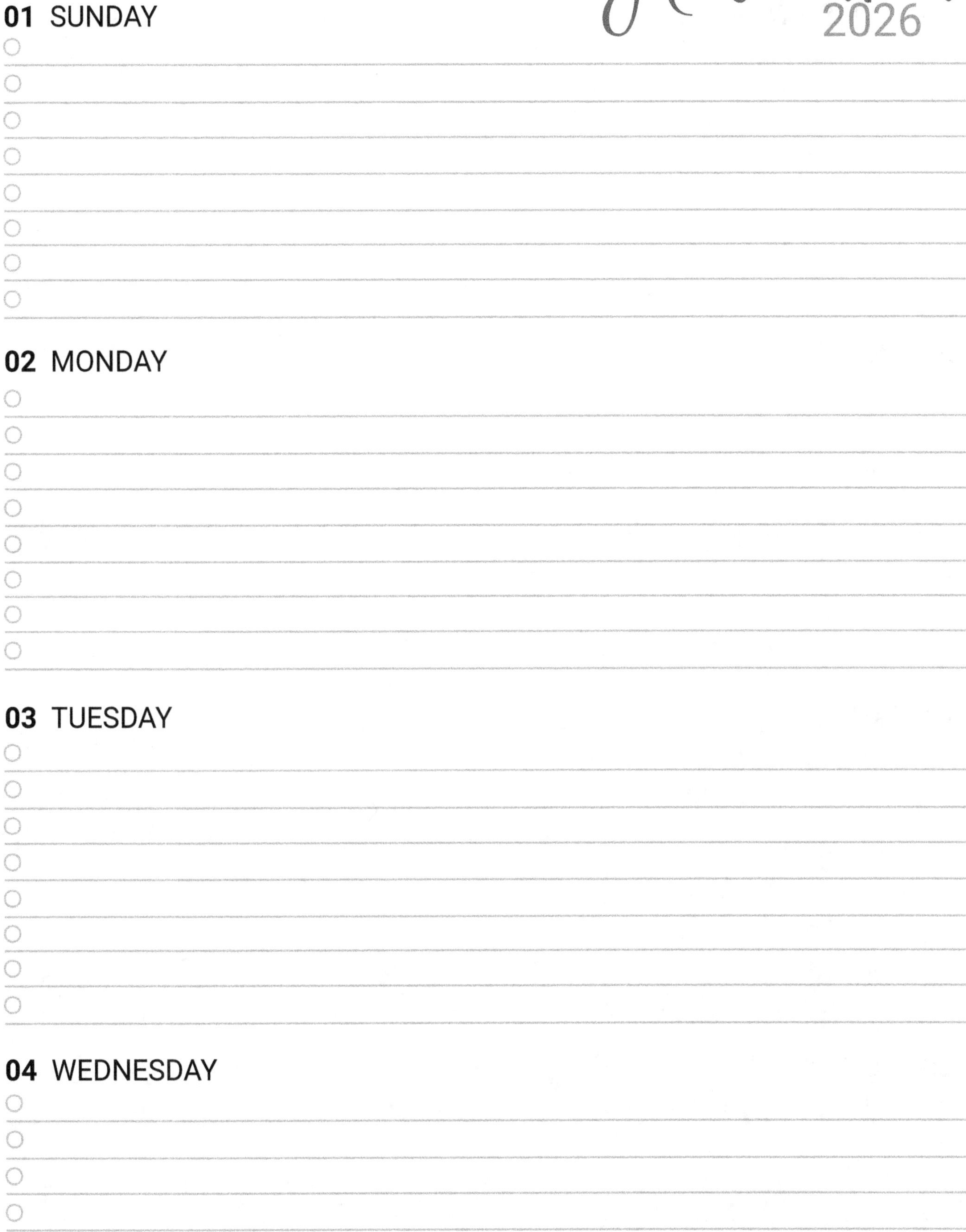

November
2026

01 SUNDAY

02 MONDAY

03 TUESDAY

04 WEDNESDAY

November
2026

05 THURSDAY

06 FRIDAY

07 SATURDAY

08 SUNDAY

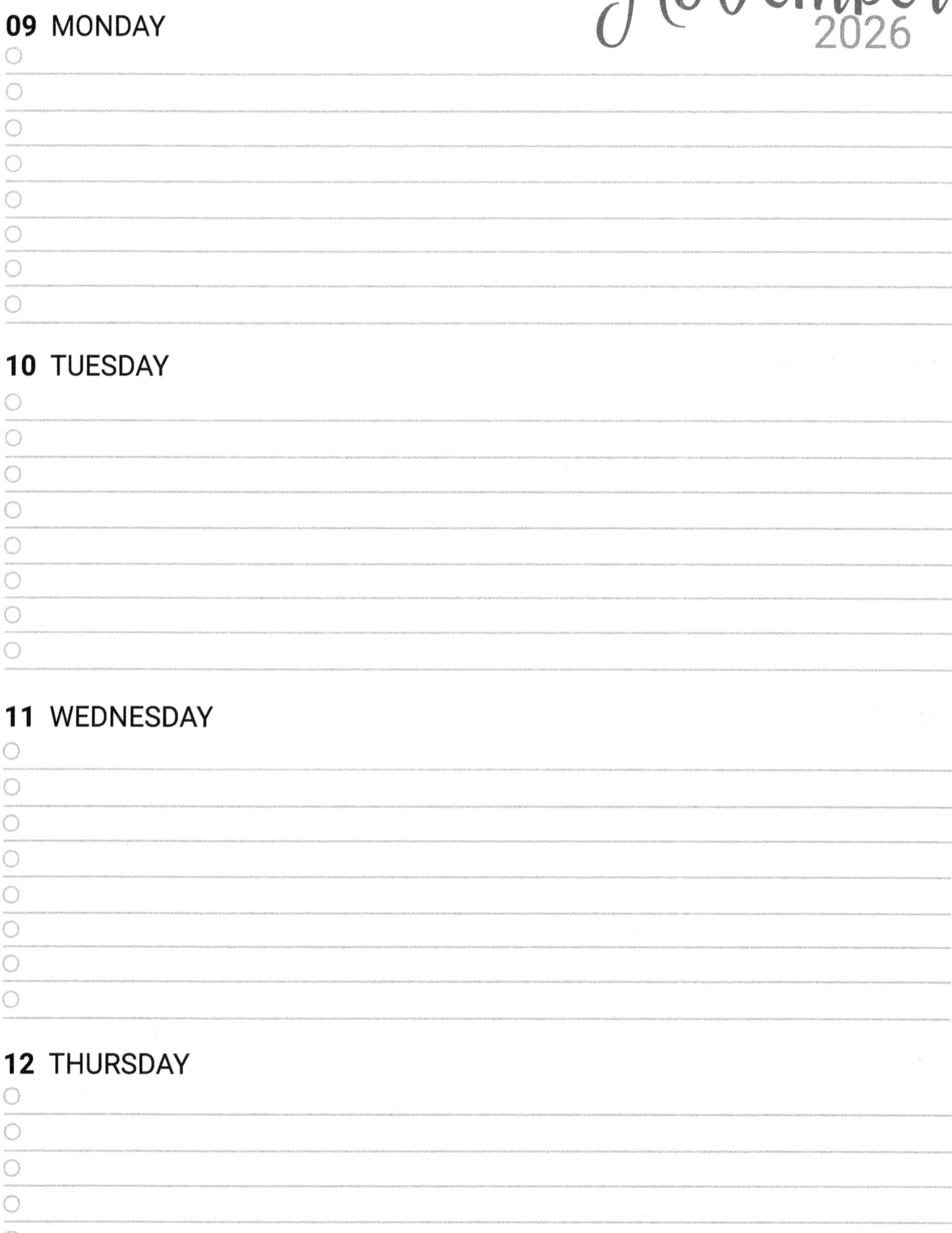

November
2026

09 MONDAY

10 TUESDAY

11 WEDNESDAY

12 THURSDAY

November
2026

13 FRIDAY

14 SATURDAY

15 SUNDAY

16 MONDAY

17 TUESDAY

18 WEDNESDAY

19 THURSDAY

20 FRIDAY

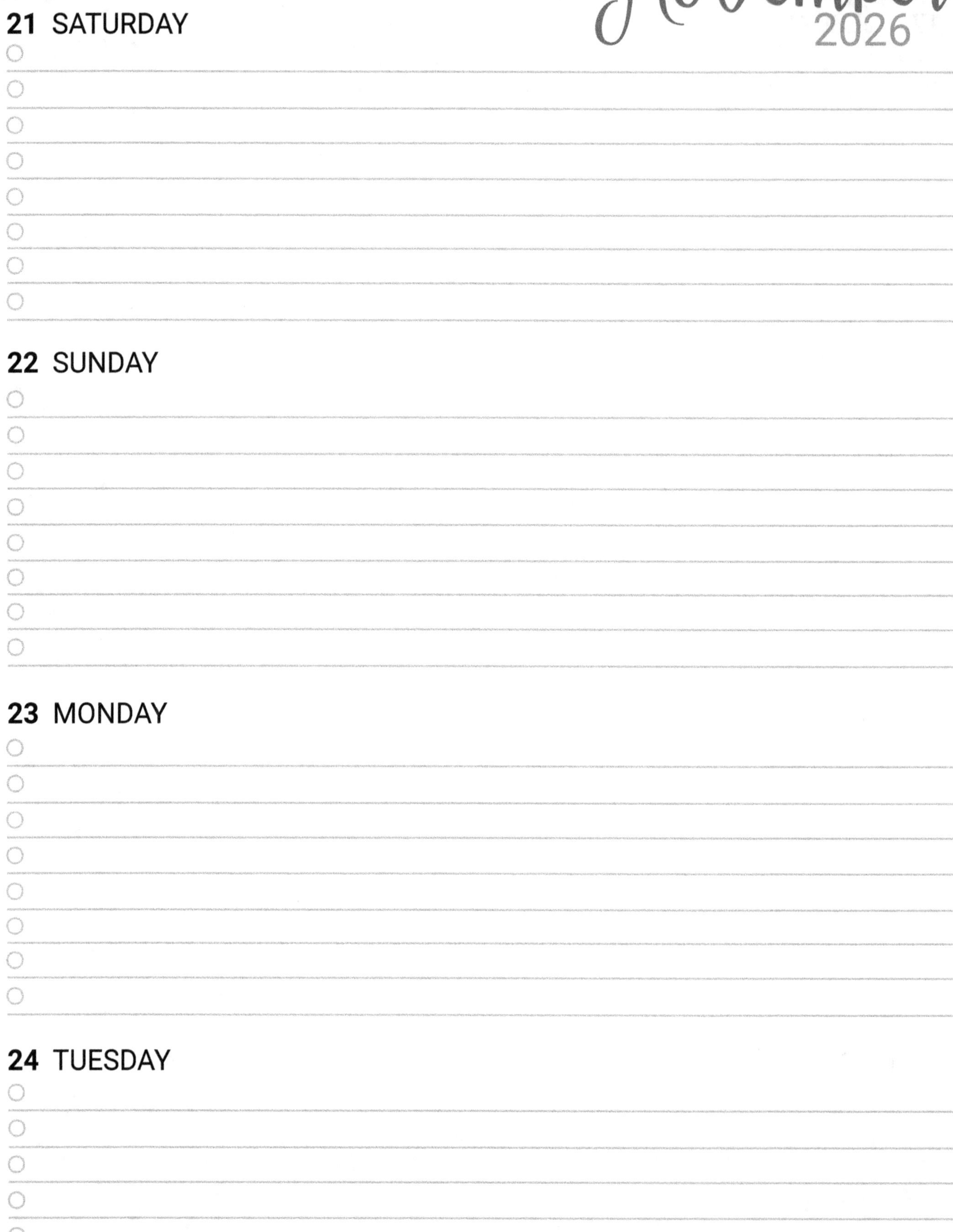

21 SATURDAY

22 SUNDAY

23 MONDAY

24 TUESDAY

25 WEDNESDAY

26 THURSDAY

27 FRIDAY

28 SATURDAY

November
2026

29 SUNDAY

30 MONDAY

NOTES

December
2026

01 TUESDAY

02 WEDNESDAY

03 THURSDAY

04 FRIDAY

December
2026

05 SATURDAY

06 SUNDAY

07 MONDAY

08 TUESDAY

09 WEDNESDAY

10 THURSDAY

11 FRIDAY

12 SATURDAY

December
2026

13 SUNDAY

14 MONDAY

15 TUESDAY

16 WEDNESDAY

December
2026

17 THURSDAY

18 FRIDAY

19 SATURDAY

20 SUNDAY

21 MONDAY

22 TUESDAY

23 WEDNESDAY

24 THURSDAY

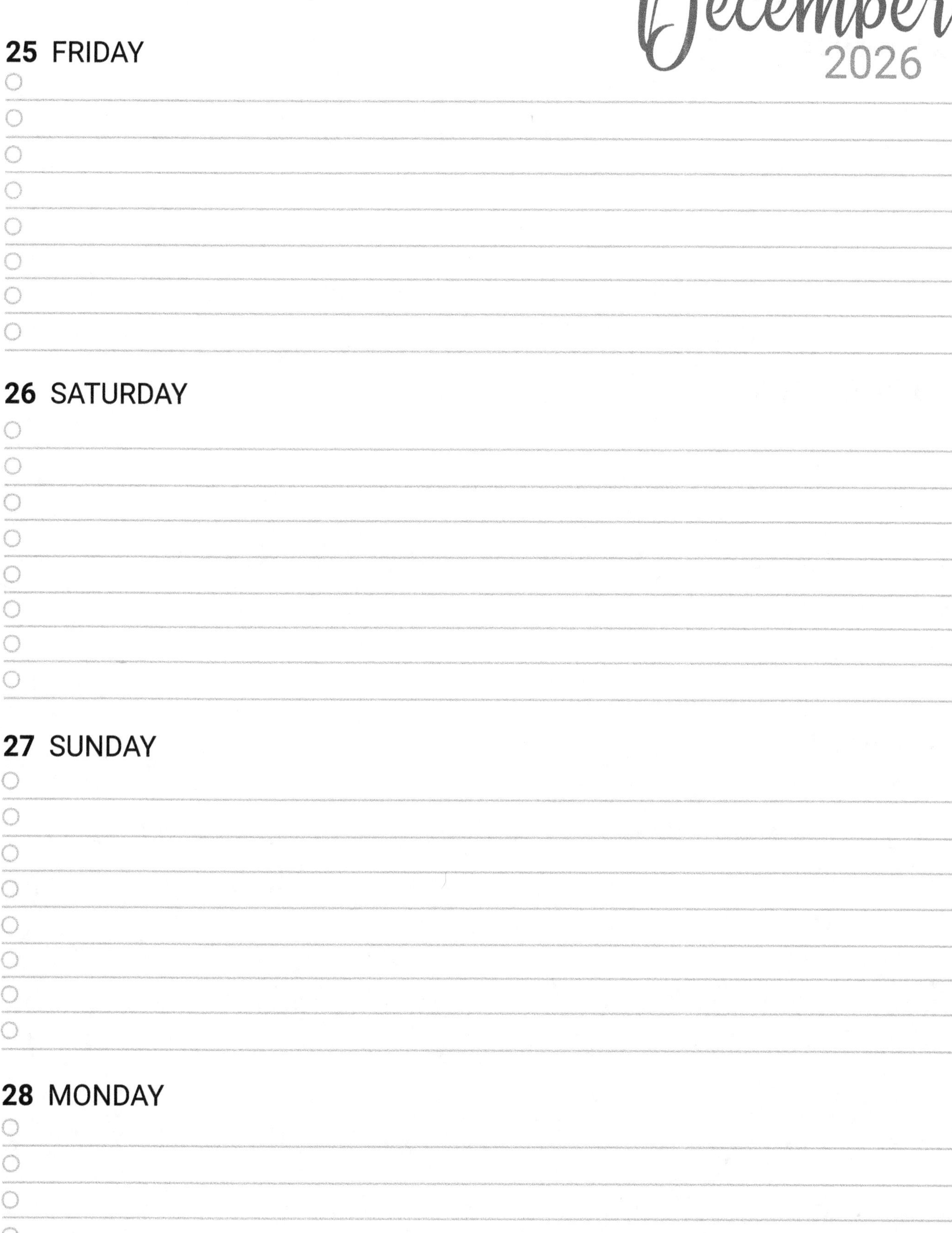

December
2026

25 FRIDAY

26 SATURDAY

27 SUNDAY

28 MONDAY

December
2026

29 TUESDAY

30 WEDNESDAY

31 THURSDAY

NOTES

www.ingramcontent.com/pod-product-compliance
Lightning Source LLC
Chambersburg PA
CBHW080517030726
47592CB00012B/3376